GW01157934

Take up Windsurfing

by
Jeremy Evans
Jeremy Evans is editor of *Boards*, the UK's leading
windsurfing magazine

SPRINGFIELD BOOKS LIMITED

Copyright © Springfield Books Limited and White Line Press
1991

ISBN 0 947655 75 1

First published 1991 by
Springfield Books Limited
Springfield House, Norman Road, Denby Dale, Huddersfield
HD8 8TH

Edited, designed and produced by
White Line Press
60 Bradford Road, Stanningley, Leeds LS28 6EF

Editors: Noel Whittall and Philip Gardner
Design: Krystyna Hewitt
Diagrams: Barry Davies

Printed and bound in Great Britain

Photographic credits
Cover photograph: © Allsport

We are grateful to *Boards* magazine and to the many
manufacturers who have supplied photographs for this book.

Take up
Windsurfing

Take up Sport

Titles in this series currently available or shortly to be published:

Contents

Introduction

Windsurfing was without doubt the fastest growing watersport of the 1980s, and shows every sign of continuing to grow rapidly throughout the 1990s.

How it started

It started simply enough when a couple of Californians, Hoyle Schweitzer and Jim Drake, hit on the idea of attaching a sail to a surfbord so that they could get over the boring process of having to paddle out to the waves. To do this they invented a rig that used a wishbone for a boom and had a universal joint attaching the mast to the board, allowing it to be inclined or rotated in any direction. This is the basis on which all windsurfers have been designed, and though it seems pretty obvious now it was a pioneering breakthrough in those early days.

Hoyle Schweitzer decided to put his idea into production in the late 1960s, but it was slow to catch on until a Dutch manufacturer decided to try selling these strange new "windsurfer" boards in Europe. They were so successful that within a few short years they were licensed to set up their own manufacturing plant, and the windsurfing explosion started.

Others were quick to copy the new idea, with Mistral and Windglider (now defunct) being among the first to produce rivals for the Windsurfer. Schweitzer had patented his idea, and over the years this led to endless legal wrangling with various people attempting to show that they had "invented" windsurfing before Schweitzer; now it's all ancient history, and the patent and Schweitzer himself, who today has little to do with the sport, are mainly forgotten.

As windsurfing (or boardsailing as it is often called) grew in popularity, it was recognised in 1977 by the International Yacht Racing Union. In most countries the national yachting association is the governing body for windsurfing; various specific windsurfing or board-sailing associations also exist. Since 1984 windsurfing has been an Olympic sport.

Windsurfing today

The countries where windsurfing flourishes most are now France, Germany and the USA, with Japan not far behind, though it's popular worldwide wherever there's sailable water. It's impossible to put figures on the overall sales of boards or numbers of participants, but a fair guesstimate is that France and Germany have well over a million windsurfers with average annual sales of around 60,000 boards in each country, as well as a great deal of money spent on all the windsurfing accessories.

Despite variable weather the sport is also hugely popular in the UK where there are more than 250,000 windsurfers. With the help of winter wetsuits enthusiasts can pursue windsurfing as a year-round pastime, with scores of sailing locations to choose from both inland and on the sea. Many of the most favoured locations are along the south coast of England and around Cornwall.

Why windsurfing?

So what is the attraction of windsurfing? It's just you, the board and the sail harnessing the power of the wind as you hiss along over the water. The costs are relatively low; you can do it almost anywhere; and there is always something new to learn, whether sailing a shorter board, going faster, exploring a new location, trying out your skill in waves, or having a go at racing.

Provided that you are able-bodied and can swim, windsurfing has no limits: all you have to do is go out and enjoy it!

Relaxed and perfectly balanced, the modern windsurfer stays in control.

The board

The windsurfing board is a tough, buoyant structure, made of a strong plastic shell filled with foam. The greater the board's volume, the more it is buoyant. It is recognisably a sailing vessel, with a pointed, slightly raised bow (the nose) and a square stern (the tail).

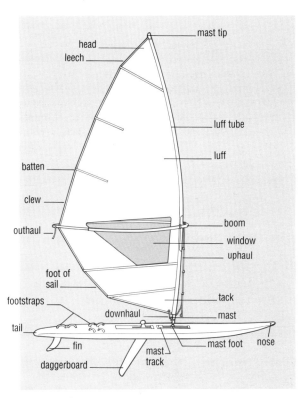

Figure 1 A typical long board and rig with all the modern windsurfing fittings. These are described in chapters 3, 7 and 9.

All boards must have a good non-slip surface on the deck, so that you don't keep sliding off!

Boards vary greatly in length, from over 370 cm to under 250 cm. Looking through windsurfing magazines you might assume that 90 per cent of boards are in fact "short boards" of around 300 cm or less. The truth is that the numbers of "long" and "short" boards are probably fairly evenly divided, but short boards tend to reflect the glitzy, glamorous side of windsurfing and hence get the lion's share of publicity and coverage.

Boards vary in length, volume and buoyancy.

In the early days of windsurfing, all boards were long. The original Windsurfer, based on an old Malibu surfboard, was around 360 cm long with a volume of 180 litres, and the boards that initially succeeded it were longer still with even more volume, giving better performance in the days when windsurfing was most enjoyable as a light-wind sport.

Things started to change with the evolution of short boards in Hawaii in the early 1980s. The main Hawaiian island of Oahu had become established as the mecca of windsurfing, principally because it was home to the young Robby Naish, who won his first windsurfer world championship at the age of 13 and from then on dominated most aspects of the sport. He and other enterprising locals began experimenting with combining short surfboards and windsurfer rigs, and with the constant strong winds and warm waters of Hawaii rapid evolution was able to take place.

Long boards

Long boards have daggerboards to stop them going sideways. Their length ranges from 320 cm to over 370 cm — mainly towards the top end — and they have sufficient volume to perform well in light winds and to carry heavier sailors. In practice this means at least 160 litres, though most are in the area of 190–220 litres; the correct volume distribution throughout the length of the board is as important as the total volume.

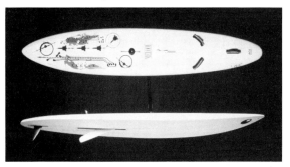

A typical long board, with daggerboard for preventing sideways drift

Long boards can be divided into categories, though as with all aspects of windsurfing there is much overlap, and divisions are never as clear as they might seem at first.

Beginner boards
The classic all-round recreational boards are ideal for beginners and family use. They are around 370 cm long with at least 200 litres of volume, and are almost invariably constructed in tough blow-moulded or roto-moulded plastics to keep the price low.

All-round funboards
A class of performance-oriented recreation boards, funboards are somewhat shorter than beginner boards at approximately 350 cm. The volume still remains high at around 180 litres, and their construction ranges from roto-moulded plastic to composites with prices varying accordingly. These boards can be recommended to any ambitious or lightweight beginner, and for general all-round use. They respond well in a good breeze.

Race boards
These are boards for experienced sailors, based on the World Cup course racing discipline, with many of the

production boards in this class developed almost directly from race prototypes. The optimum length is usually around 370 cm, with 195–245 litres volume. These dimensions are similar to those of beginner boards, but race boards have specialist design, construction and detailing. All these boards have a big fin and daggerboard, a mass of footstraps, and a long sliding mast track as standard. They have fairly large sails (up to 7.5 sq m), though even larger specialist sails are available for experts to use in light winds. Race boards are generally of composite construction, which is most effective at making these relatively large, long boards both light and stiff. Prices are high.

320s

320s are — not surprisingly — 320 cm long. They are the shortest boards with daggerboards; the next step down has crossed the boundary and is definitely a "short board". As with all these categories, there is great variety in size and shape — some 320s are actually closer to 330 cm, and volumes range from 150 to 190 litres, with performance that is correspondingly more suitable for moderate or for stronger winds. A very ambitious beginner weighing in at under 65 kg could certainly consider one of these boards; their light-wind performance will never equal that of longer, more voluminous boards, but once you've progressed to stronger winds they should be more fun and more responsive.

Short boards

Short boards do not have daggerboards. They are too short to build them into the hull, and in any case they have no need of them. A short board is designed to be sailed only in planing conditions of 10 knots (Force 3–4) and above (see page 27), and relies on its speed and the grip of its fin to power upwind without drifting sideways.

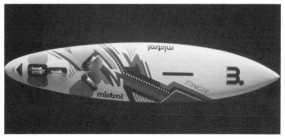

A short board. These are 3 metres or less in length, and do not have a daggerboard.

A short board is no use in non-planing conditions — if there are no white horses on the water, sailing one is a waste of time. If it has enough volume it will support you, but it will make slow and painful progress downwind (and little if any at all upwind), and all the long boards will streak past. Consequently a short board is not for beginners. Given the right conditions it is possible to learn on one, but you would have to wait for the wind every time you sailed and would miss out on all the fun that long boards can provide.

Short boards do, however, give windsurfing a second dimension. They are for when you can handle a long board with confidence in light, moderate or strong winds, a stage that could be achieved from zero in just a few months with the right instruction, application, some natural ability, and a fair amount of luck with the weather. More likely it will take quite a bit longer. When you've got there, the classic short board to start with is the 295.

The 295

The biggest short boards are around 295 cm or longer, with relatively high volume (up to 130 litres). Compared with long boards they are unstable and "tippy", but nothing like as much as the remainder of the short board classes. All constructions are available, at correspondingly varied prices.

Slaloms

Slalom is at present the most popular label for a short board, based closely or not-so-closely on World-Cup-style slalom competition. Some 295s are dubbed slalom, but most slaloms are in the 260–290 cm range with around 100 litres of volume, which brings most of them close to becoming sinkers (see page 53). These are demanding boards to sail, requiring a high level of expertise. All the principal manufacturers produce them.

Wave boards

A wave board is a design purely for sailing in waves — riding them, gybing on them, and jumping off them. The pure wave board is a specialist tool, very short and with very low volume, for real experts to play on. There are also compromise designs called "wave-slaloms".

Speed boards

The most specialised short boards of all are the pencil-slim speed boards with minimal volume that are designed for batting along a speed course at 40 knots and more. Almost all are specially made custom boards, definitely for experts only.

3

Windsurfing rigs

The wind and the sail

When the wind fills a correctly trimmed sail and shapes it into a curve, the air flow separates and passes on either side. On the leeward side (the one further from the wind) the air flow is faster, because it has to go round the outside of the curve, and the result is a reduction in air pressure. On the windward side of the sail (closest to the sailor and the wind) there is a high-pressure area which pushes towards the low pressure, thus creating drive in the sail.

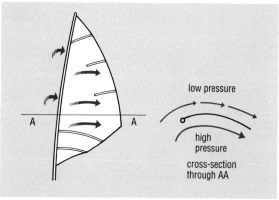

Figure 2 The airflow past the sail

This drive is turned into forward drive by the shape of the sail, the shape of the board which must resist the natural tendency to be pushed sideways, and the sailor's skill in handling it. When rig, board and sailor are in balance, the windsurfer will sail forwards with minimal sideways drift (leeway), since the Centre of Effort (CE) in the sail — the point where the wind's force can be thought of as being concentrated —

balances with the Centre of Lateral Resistance (CLR) in the board, which is the point about which it is designed to turn. On long boards it is the daggerboard, aided by the tail fin, which chiefly provides the lateral resistance.

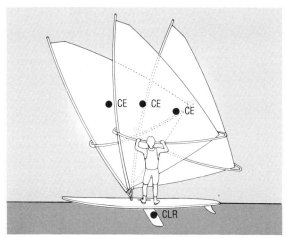

Figure 3 The principles of steering. When the CE balances the CLR, the board sails straight. Lean the rig forward to turn away from the wind; lean it back to turn into the wind.

In light winds steering is accomplished by leaning the rig forward so that the CE is in front of the CLR and pushes the bow away from the wind (bearing away), or leaning the rig back so the CE is behind the CLR and pushes the stern away from the wind (heading up). These are the basics of sailing in a straight line and changing direction which the beginner must master.

In stronger winds everything changes. While a yacht heels *away* from the wind, a windsurfer heels its rig *into* the wind with the sailor hanging underneath. This is a much more efficient technique. The board stays flat on the water as it is designed to do, and the pull in the sail helps to lift it up off the water, making it travel faster as it skims across the surface. Steering in stronger winds is usually achieved by "footsteering" — see chapter 9.

Figure 4 When the wind blows the sailor leans back, supported by the rig. His weight balances the power of the sail; the push of the mastfoot is controlled by the push of his feet.

Like a yacht, a windsurfer must change to smaller sails as the wind gets stronger. The "standard" size with most windsurfers is about 6 sq m, which is suitable for all light winds, while for stronger winds a couple of smaller sizes will be necessary — 5 sq m and 4 sq m for very strong winds are popular choices.

Sail selection doesn't stop there, for sails are made in all sizes from as small as 3 sq m to as large as 7.5 sq m and even bigger. Many of these are designed as specialist sails — the very small ones for advanced wave-sailors and the very big ones for racers — but for beginners the choice is useful as you can always find a size to suit your ability and stature.

A modern high-performance rig with full-length battens for stability

Types of sail

A windsurfing sail is made of Dacron (woven polyester) or Mylar (polyester film) panels cut to specific shapes and sewn or taped together. Some of these panels will be transparent to act as windows. Dacron is cheaper and more hard wearing, and perfectly adequate sails can be found among the cheaper ranges. There is no need to go to the most expensive types of sail until you really are an expert who demands Porsche-style excellence and prices!

The simplest kind of sail has no fibreglass battens to support it. Consequently it is light for learning, but soon loses its shape and becomes unstable when the wind picks up. A sail with battens is more powerful and much more stable. Full-length battens are used to support extra area in the bottom (foot) and side (roach), and if there are five or more battens they can transform the sail into something that performs like a solid wing.

Most of these sails with full-length battens are called "rotationals" because the leading edge of the sail rotates around the mast, allowing you to set the sail on the leeward side where it is aerodynamically most efficient.

The best sails to learn with are probably "soft" sails which have full-length battens supporting the top and bottom, with shorter leech battens in between. They tend to be lighter and more responsive than fully battened sails, and so they are easily handled if it's not too windy.

Today's windsurfer sails are light as well as strong!

Rig components

Aside from the sail, there are three principal rig components:

The mast fits inside the luff tube of the sail. Standard masts are 4.65 or 4.85 metres long, and the most popular are made in glassfibre, which is light and has the correct bending characteristics. Aluminium masts are preferred for racing, but tend to be more expensive.

The mast foot (or mast base) fits in the bottom of the mast. It is connected to a rubber universal joint (UJ) which in turn connects to the board, fitting into a sliding mast track or into a fixed socket. This universal joint allows the rig to be inclined at any angle. The mast foot may also include an adjustable mast extension, or one can be added if the mast proves to be too short for the sail.

The boom is made up of two aluminium tubes, shaped like a wishbone, with moulded plastic end-fittings. The front end-fitting attaches to the mast at around shoulder height; in the old days this was done by a rope lashing, but now a simple mechanical clamp which gives a tight fit is more usual. The outhaul line of the sail is attached to the other end-fitting, and can be adjusted as necessary to vary the fulness of the sail. Most booms are adjustable in length so that they can be used with different-sized sails.

4

Windsurfing accessories

Go into any windsurfing shop, and there are any number of accessories. Some are vital; some are useful; others are pure luxuries. As a beginner, you should get the most vital items first.

Clothing

In any cold climate you *must* have a wetsuit. Apart from the basic fact that it is uncomfortable to go windsurfing if you're cold, it is also dangerous. Wind chill rapidly lowers body temperature, as do repeated falls into the water. Together they can produce a condition called hypothermia which can incapacitate the sailor and in extreme cases can lead to unconsciousness and death.

A wetsuit will prevent such problems, though you must have the right wetsuit for the season. All wetsuits are made of neoprene rubber panels — go for "double-lined" neoprene which is best for wear and tear. A wetsuit works by trapping a thin layer of water between itself and your body. This water layer soon warms up, and together with the neoprene it provides very good insulation against heat loss. They all keep the wind out, but how much water the suit keeps out will depend on the fit at neck, wrists and ankles and the type of stitching. The best wetsuits are called "steamers" — they have a watertight "blind stitch" and are consequently the most expensive. The rest will let small amounts of cold water flush through every time you fall, which doesn't matter in the summer but will rapidly cool you down in the cold months.

A wetsuit needs to be a close fit, which means the neoprene must stretch when you do. Trying on a suit for size before you buy is very important. Thinner neoprene will obviously be the stretchiest of all, but is really only suitable for the summer; thicker neoprene is more rigid, but is tougher and makes a warmer winter suit. Some compromise is called for, and don't get too warm a suit or you'll find yourself overheating.

A neoprene wetsuit is a must to keep you warm.

The most popular style of suit used to be the "long john" — a one-piece with long legs and no arms. The attraction is that a bolero-style top can be worn over the long john when the weather gets cold, but this style of suit has now been superseded by the more stylish short-sleeve and long-sleeve suits illustrated, which are warmer and generally perform better.

Depending on where you sail, you may also need foot protection. All kinds of rubber and neoprene boots and shoes are available. They must be comfortable, they must stay on, and they must have a good grip. In practice this is seldom a problem, as most windsurfing shoes and boots will grip better than your bare feet.

Gloves are seldom necessary unless you sail in very cold weather. Most booms have a soft rubber grip which is kind on the hands, and if freezing fingers are your problem it's unfortunate that no manufacturer has really cracked the problem of producing a good wind-surfing glove. A watertight neoprene mit is probably the best bet while learning, but proves clumsy once you're more expert.

Buoyancy aid
A buoyancy aid is a waistcoat containing soft flotation foam. You should always wear one while learning to windsurf, even if you are a strong swimmer.

Harnesses and harness lines

The windsurfing harness has a hook positioned at about waist height which lets you hang from a line on either side of the boom. It's a tremendous advantage for experienced windsurfers, since it allows you to take the strain of holding on to the sail with your whole body, not just with your arms.

However the harness is not for beginners. It is pointless using one in light winds, and no windsurfer should attempt to learn to sail with one until he can handle a board confidently in moderate and quite strong winds. When that time comes a variety of styles are available — chest, waist and seat harnesses. The seat harness is generally the most popular. For more information, see chapter 9.

Using the harness takes the strain off your arms.

Whatever the type of harness, make sure it fits well without chafing. If anything goes wrong while sailing — if you fall in, for example — just release the harness line (a quick-release fastening helps).

Roof rack and straps

Unless you are fortunate enough to live by the waterside, you will need a car roof rack and straps to tie on the board and rig. The simple, original Thule roof rack has probably not been bettered, but those with gutterless cars may need to look further for a rack to suit their particular model. If this incorporates some sort of locking device, so much the better.

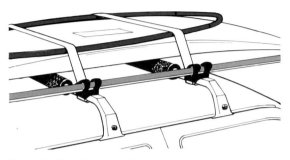

Figure 5 Boards should be placed deck down on the roof rack, with the nose pointing forwards. They should be as far back on the rack as possible. Use proper roof rack straps or purpose-made clamps, and check that the board is very firmly secured, with no sharp edges cutting into the straps. The mast is best carried in a separate holder; the boom can be secured on top of the board or carried inside the car.

The racks on a car roof must be positioned as far apart as possible. The board is usually best placed deck down, with the boom on top and the mast alongside. A second board can go on top of the first, and with care four 370-cm boards can be carried safely on a small family car. Do make sure the rack and the rack straps are correctly fastened. Every year there are accidents with racks and boards coming off car roofs; tighten the rack correctly and use a secure technique for strapping down the board, and you will have no problem.

Insurance

If you own a board, you should have insurance — third-party at least to protect yourself and anyone you might inadvertently run into. Comprehensive cover for windsurfers is reasonably priced, and is a wise precaution since most countries suffer from a certain amount of board theft, particularly from car roof racks. Note that most insurance companies will only cover you for theft if your board is locked to the roof rack.

5

Learning to windsurf

As with any sport, you need some help to learn to windsurf. If you prefer to teach yourself, this book will introduce you to the basics and get you onto the water. Read what it says about the basic techniques; try them on the beach or water; then read the book again. You should be a reasonably competent swimmer before you begin.

You may have a friend who offers to teach you. This is fair enough if he's patient enough to teach you properly, and good enough at windsurfing not to pass on his own mistakes and poor technique. However, for a solid grounding it's better to go on a professionally run windsurfing course — the boards and all necessary equipment will be provided; you'll be taught to do things properly; the cost is reasonable; and it doesn't take much time.

> Windsurfing is unusual among watersports in being relatively unsuitable for disabled people. Its athletic demands are considerable, and in general you do need to be reasonably able-bodied and fit. As always, there are exceptions: some one-armed people, for example, have taken up windsurfing with the aid of suitable equipment.
>
> If you are disabled and keen to have a go at windsurfing, do take qualified advice first: in the UK, the Water Sports Division of the British Sports Association for the Disabled will be able to help.

RYA courses

In the UK the RYA (address on page 55) has an excellent system of windsurfing courses ranging from beginner to expert. These are for anyone over 14 years of age. The basic beginner course lasts some eight hours — usually over two days, provided that the weather allows — and aims to give a thorough grounding in theory and safety, before putting you on the water and teaching you to sail out and back again.

Certificates are issued for each level succesfully completed, and the RYA has almost 200 recognised schools offering their courses in the UK, as well as a handful in the warmer waters of the Mediterranean for those who choose to combine learning to windsurf with a holiday. The average cost of a course is less than £50, with all equipment, proper changing facilities, a qualified instructor and safety cover provided.

The RYA also runs a Junior Windsurfing Scheme aimed at youngsters aged 8–14, with Junior Fleets (special small boards and small sails) and tuition available at centres in the UK.

Making progress

The RYA has divided windsurfing into five levels which chart your windsurfing progress. A similar scheme is used by windsurfing authorities in other countries.

Level 1: Learning
This includes:

- rigging
- carrying and launching the board and rig
- sailing, steering and stopping
- tacking and gybing
- self-rescue and safety
- sailing theory
- understanding weather conditions.

Level 2: Improving

- the beach start
- improved reaching, running and beating
- using the daggerboard
- the right stance
- better tacking and gybing
- understanding the rig
- fitness
- rights of way
- tides
- windsurfing competition.

Level 3: Stronger winds

- uphauling and starting in stronger winds
- stance, harness, footstraps and footsteering
- fast tacks and gybes
- railing
- types of harnesses

Level 4: Funboard techniques

- launching and landing in waves and the waterstart
- better speed, closing the slot, using the mast track
- carve gybes
- hi-tech sails and construction
- rips and undertows
- fast planing and spin-out.

Level 5: Advanced funboard techniques

- advanced waterstarts and launching in surf
- wave jumping, riding and transitions
- short-board gybes
- short-board rescues and surf survival
- short-board design
- wave and speed contests.

The duck gybe is an advanced technique which combines the carve gybe with ducking beneath the sail. When performed well, it looks most impressive!

Few windsurfers will stick rigidly to the RYA's levels, although they do chart a sensible progression. Many choose to transfer their affections to a short board when they can barely handle a long board; apart from many other drawbacks this restricts them to only being able to sail in stronger winds.

How fast you will progress depends on your own aptitude, how frequently you can get out on the water, and the conditions. A solid fortnight of warm water and good winds could set you up better than a frustrating summer of missed opportunites with too much or too little wind, and for this reason a specialist windsurfing holiday in a warm climate is usually an excellent way to get started. From there you could progress quite rapidly, mastering stronger winds and the harness by the end of the first season and perhaps moving on to racing or short-board sailing the season beyond.

6

Windsurfing in safety

You can windsurf anywhere there is wind and water, so long as it is legal. However, as with any waterborne activities, some locations are dangerous, and safety and common sense are prime considerations when choosing where to go windsurfing.

If possible, always sail in company: this is much safer than windsurfing on your own.

In the early stages of learning there are a number of things which could put you off for good: if it's freezing cold, blowing too hard, flat calm with no wind at all, or if there are waves that knock you off the board every few seconds.

Wind direction

However, the principal danger when learning is being blown away from the shore and not being able to get back. An *offshore* wind gets progressively stronger the further out you go, and as you find you can't cope you spend more and more time in the water, getting blown where you don't want to go at an ever-increasing speed. The end result is that you must be rescued.

An offshore wind is unsatisfactory for the beginner (near the shore the wind is likely to be very gusty as it blows past trees or houses), but an *onshore* wind can be as bad. The wind will heap up waves, and if the bottom shelves sharply these can build up into surf with a fierce undertow: dangerous conditions like these can result in broken gear and bruised egos.

So when possible you should go for the ideal wind direction, which is *sideshore*, blowing from left to right or right to left across the launch area.

Figure 6 Rescue me! If you can't sail, it's possible to roll up the rig and paddle home. The standard distress signal is to raise and lower your arms.

Tides

When sailing on the sea you should also be aware of tides. Conditions near the shore can differ greatly between low and high tide, with big waves "dumping" powerfully on the beach at high tide while being comparatively harmless at low tide. However, low tide may mean you have to carry your board and rig for several hundred metres over the sand or through mud, so that the right compromise solution always depends on having some local knowledge. You should also be aware that tides can flow a good deal faster than you can swim, particularly through channels, near river mouths and round headlands. All of these are potential danger areas; to make sure you don't fall foul of them, get some local knowledge from experienced windsurfers before you go out.

The weather

Windsurfers are interested in wind, and once past the learning stage they want plenty of it. Wind and weather are also vital safety considerations, and it's important to keep in touch with weather forecasts and to have enough basic knowledge to interpret them. Few if any weather forecasts are specifically designed for windsurfers, but you will learn most from weather maps showing isobars and predicted wind speeds, and from any inshore water forecasts that are available. In most places you can also telephone for pre-recorded local coastal area forecasts, or perhaps best of all phone up a Weather Centre to get personal advice about the weather and windsurfing prospects.

Wind is created by differences in atmospheric pressure. In some cases this produces a wind which blows consistently day after day — the seasonal trade winds which blow through the Canaries, the Caribbean and Hawaii are a great favourite with windsurfers. A more localised phenomenon occurs when the sun heats up the land more quickly than the sea, creating a low-pressure area which sucks air inland. This creates an onshore wind which can build up along the coastline in summertime, starting at around midday, peaking by mid-afternoon, and dropping in the early evening. In hot countries the wind produced can be very strong.

The Beaufort Scale

Windsurfers, like other sailors, talk about knots and measure the wind in Forces. Knots are nautical miles per hour, and a nautical mile is 2,025 yards (1.85 km) as opposed to the land mile of 1,760 yards — so a knot is 1.15 land miles per hour. The Beaufort Scale which measures the force of the wind was invented by Admiral Beaufort in 1805 with descriptions for the open sea. Windsurfing should never be done far away from the coast, so the descriptions should be modified to suit the surroundings. With experience the wind force can then be guesstimated with reasonable accuracy, though an anemometer is the only sure way of getting it right — all windsurfers are liable to exaggerate!

Force 0 1 knot or less. Calm, mirror-like sea. No use for windsurfing.

Force 1 1–3 knots. Light air. Gentle scaly ripples. OK for drifting, but too light for fun.

Force 2 4–6 knots. Light breeze. Small wavelets, which may have glassy crests but these will not break. Very good for learning.

Force 3 7–10 knots. Gentle breeze. Large wavelets. Fine for learning without the wavelets which are unlikely to affect sheltered water.

Force 4 11–16 knots. Moderate breeze. Waves becoming longer with white horses. Windsurfers start to move really fast. Too windy for most beginners. Force 4 is the standard minimum for international funboard racing.

Force 5 17–21 knots. Fresh breeze. Moderate waves with white horses and possible occasional spray. Great weather for short boards.

Be prepared, and know what the weather will bring. Force 6 conditions like these are definitely for experts only.

Force 6 22–27 knots. Strong breeze. Large waves forming, with extensive white crests and spray. Only for experts.

Force 7 28–33 knots. Near gale. Sea heaps up and foam from breaking waves is blown in streaks. Only for real experts.

Force 8 34–40 knots. Gale. Moderately high waves. The edges of crests break into spindrift. The limit for experts.

Force 9 41–46 knots. Severe gale. High waves. Confused breaking crests.

Force 10 48–55 knots. Violent storm. Exceptionally high waves hiding ships from view. Sea covered in white foam.

Rules of the road

Like all waterborne craft, windsurfers are governed by "rules of the road" designed to prevent collision. This is a necessity. Windsurfers can travel so fast that collision is potentially dangerous — imagine two boards crashing head-on at 25 knots! Common sense is also required, and the following rules and guidelines should be adhered to:

● Never get in the way of commercial craft, and treat any motorboats or yachts with respect — if they're negotiating a channel, they have right of way.

● When two sailing craft meet, starboard tack has right of way over port tack.

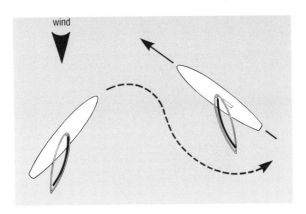

Figure 7 The board on the right has right of way because it is on its starboard tack. The board on the port tack has to give way.

● When two sailing craft converge on the same tack, the one to leeward has right of way.

● The overtaking craft keeps clear.

● Don't assume that other sailors and boat users know the rules of the road or abide by them.

● On a windsurfer it is easy to change course; on a larger vessel it is not. In many cases it makes sense for the windsurfer to give way.

Swimmers

Windsurfers should also take great care on crowded beaches, both on shore and on the water. Left lying around, a windsurfer and its rig takes up a lot of space, and an upturned skeg is potentially hazardous for children playing nearby. Don't hog the beach; leave your kit out of the way, and when you carry it to and from the water take care not to swipe anyone, shower them with sand, or cause any other annoyance.

In the water close to the shore there may well be swimmers. Sailing a board among them is not easy, and the onus is on the windsurfer to keep away. Remember that a board in this situation is potentially lethal, and a number of fatalities have been caused in this way. On some popular beaches there are marked "lanes" for launching, while the rest of the beach is banned to windsurfers. So long as the windsurfers get a fair deal, this is a good solution which keeps boards and swimmers apart in the interests of both.

7

Rigging

With a few exceptions, all windsurfers are basically the same (see chapters 2 and 3). Once you've learned to rig one you should be able to rig them all.

Putting it together

Putting a new board together is comparatively simple:

Tail fin (skeg)
Virtually all fins have a lug on the trailing edge which slides into the fin box; the leading edge is then held down by a bolt which screws into a plate inside the box. Sliding the fin to the back of the box will make the board more directionally stable; sliding it to the front will make the board more manoeuvrable.

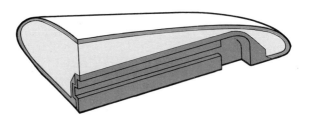

Figure 8 A cutaway of the tail section of a modern board. Note the skeg-box reinforcement necessary to withstand the massive sideways strain.

Footstraps
Don't use footstraps until you have mastered the basics of windsurfing. They are only of use in winds over Force 4, and when you are learning they clutter the deck and get in the way. Leave them off until you're ready for them; then you can screw them into the holes provided.

Daggerboard

The daggerboard is inserted vertically in its case. When sailing it should go up and down with light foot pressure, but should be a tight enough fit not to float up of its own accord. There are normally adjustable lugs to prevent this.

Mast track

Lock the mast track in about the midway position, or wherever you find it most comfortable, while learning. Don't start to play with it until you've mastered Force 4 and more.

Chapter 9 gives more information about using these pieces of equipment.

A perfectly set sail with all the control lines tensioned

Rigging the sail

The sail is normally rigged and unrigged every time you go sailing. With practice this should be no more than a five-minute operation that should follow a basic sequence:

1 Slide the mast up the luff tube of the sail.

2 Push the mastfoot into the base of the mast. With a big sail an extension may be necessary to increase the length of the mast.

3 Attach the downhaul line to the mastfoot.

4 Attach the boom at the sail cutout (window) position, which should be around shoulder height when standing on the board; some prefer it a little higher, others a little lower. Most modern booms have a mechanical clamp system which fits tightly round the mast and can easily be adjusted. Older booms have a rope inhaul with various methods of getting a tight fit.

5 Insert any battens and tension them.

6 Attach the outhaul line to the end of the boom and tension it.

7 Attach the uphaul rope to the boom and mastfoot. (This is always left attached to the boom.)

8 Tension the downhaul, outhaul and battens until the sail takes up its correct shape, with plenty of camber (curve) and no creases. If there are vertical creases you probably need more outhaul or less downhaul or more batten tension; if there are horizontal creases you need more downhaul or less outhaul. In modern sails the downhaul controls most of the shape, which is cut to match the bend of the mast. Outhaul and batten tension is for fine tuning achieved by light pressure; the downhaul requires a pulley system giving at least a 4:1 force ratio to get the necessary tension, and should be pulled down so that the bottom of the sail comes close to the deck.

Carrying the board and rig

In recent years boards have become much lighter, and so are easier to carry. The easiest method of carrying is to hold the board side-on to your hip, with one hand holding the mast track and the other in the daggerboard case. Take care that a gust doesn't catch you and "weathercock" the board.

You can travel anywhere with your board!

The rig can be carried at hip height or over your head. Keep the mast at right angles to the wind (with the boom pointing into the wind) so that it powers the rig and helps carry it for you. There's a knack to this, and care should be taken so that you don't lose control or let the rig blow out of your hands.

When you move to short-board sailing, you will notice that sailors are able to carry board and rig together. This is because the board is comparatively short, light, and is easily carried by the power in the rig. The sailor is then able to launch straight into the water with minimum fuss.

Launching — doing it like this requires a fair bit of experience!

8

Basic sailing

To take your first steps in windsurfing, choose a day of light winds (Force 1–3) with flat water, avoiding an offshore wind. Be sure someone on land is keeping an eye on you, and that you can get back unassisted if you find sailing the board is beyond you.

First steps

Launch the board by dragging it and the rig into shallow water, and try balancing on it. Then plug and lock the rig into the mast track; put the daggerboard fully down; and with the wind behind you stand up with your feet either side of the mastfoot, and start pulling the rig up with the uphaul.

Figure 9 With the wind behind you, uphaul the rig with bent legs and a straight back.

At first this seems like heavy work — the wind is holding the sail down and the mast tube is full of water — so while learning a small sail makes it easier. You should keep your back straight and bend your knees, using your legs to counteract the weight of the rig. Gradually haul it up hand over hand, pausing to keep your balance. With the rig partly raised you will be able to try the basics of steering the board — rake the rig forward and the board will steer away from the wind; rake the rig back and it will head up towards the wind.

Figure 10 Get your balance and a steady grip (**1**), then pull the rig over towards the wind (**2**), before pulling in the boom with your back hand (**3**). Keep the rig angled forward, and you will be sailing!

When the rig is fully raised you can let it blow like a flag, with the wind at right angles to the board. This is the starting position, by which time most beginners will have fallen in a few times already. Never mind — regain your balance and try again. Then place your front hand on the mast just below the boom, using it to pull the mast towards you and across your body as you swivel round to face forward. This prevents the board from luffing up into the wind. To complete the manoeuvre, place your back hand and then your front hand on the boom about shoulder-width apart. Then pull in with your back hand to put some power into the sail.

The board will start moving forwards, gathering speed as you pull in on the rig. If you want to change direction away from the wind you angle the rig forward; to head up into the wind you angle the rig back.

Figure 11 To head up into the wind rake the sail back; to turn away from it angle it forwards.

Beating and tacking

For obvious reasons you can't sail directly into the wind. However, you can sail as close as possible to the wind, sailing a zigzag course which will in effect take you directly towards it. Each zigzag requires a *tack* — changing from starboard tack (when the wind comes from the right side) to port tack (when the wind comes from the left side) or vice versa. This process of tacking to windward is called *beating*.

To tack, you angle the rig back so that the nose of the board heads up into the wind. When it points directly into the wind, you have to move round the front of the mast to get to the other side. You then incline the rig forward and pull in on the boom to make the board bear away on the new tack.

Figure 12 A windsurfer makes progress upwind by zigzagging — the correct term is tacking.

When you get a little more experience, reaching in strong winds is what windsurfing is all about.

Reaching

Reaching, when the wind blows across the board, is the fastest way of sailing and also the most relaxing. It is divided into:

- close reaching (with the wind diagonally ahead)
- beam reaching (with the wind at right angles to the board)
- broad reaching (with the wind diagonally behind), which in strong winds is the fastest course of all, allowing maximum power in the sail to be transmitted into maximum forward speed with minimum sideways drift.

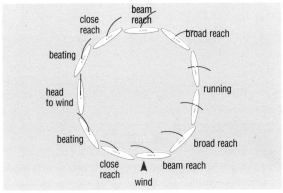

Figure 13 The points of sailing, from beam reach via running to beating

Running and gybing

Running is sailing "before the wind", with the wind directly behind you. In practice windsurfers seldom choose to sail on a downwind "run", because it is unstable and (contrary to what you might expect) comparatively slow. However, gybing — which is tacking on a downwind course — is a fast way of changing from reach to reach, and is the common method of changing tacks on short boards which are too small to be tacked in the conventional manner — if you attempted to move round the front of the mast, the bow would sink into the water under you.

To gybe in light winds, the rig is leaned over to windward (into the wind) until the board bears right away onto the new course. When the wind starts to come from the other side you let go of the boom with the back hand, allowing the rig to flick round onto the new side; be ready to catch it and continue sailing.

9

Stronger winds

Windsurfers talk of a "Force 4 barrier" which beginners come up against. Labelling it Force 4 is a generalisation, but the fact is that as the wind gets stronger everything happens much more quickly — shooting across the water in a Force 4 is very different from drifting along in a Force 2, and windsurfing in Force 6 is another thing altogether! Strong winds are handled by good technique and equipment. Reasonable fitness is important too, but unless you want to be a top competition sailor there is no call for exceptional strength or endurance.

Equipment

You need the right size sail for the wind conditions. Taken to extremes, this could mean having a "quiver" of eight sails (the minimum a World Cup sailor requires) or even more. For general use, however, three good fully battened sails will suffice 99 per cent of the time — a sail around 6 sq m or bigger for light winds; around 5 sq m for Force 4; and around 4 sq m for Force 6. There are no hard and fast rules for when you change down — a tall, heavyweight sailor would obviously hold down a big sail in stronger winds than a short featherweight would, though both would probably be able to sail at much the same speed.

Force 4 and more is also when short boards come on the scene; they will perform sluggishly in anything much lighter, but once you've got the hang of them they tend to be much easier to control than long boards in strong winds and waves, because their small size and light weight make them responsive. However, before trying your luck on a short board you should become fully proficient at mastering the daggerboard, mast tack, footstraps and harness on a long board.

Daggerboard
In light winds you can leave the daggerboard down, which makes the board more stable.

In stronger winds you need it down when sailing upwind to prevent the board from drifting sideways. However, the way the rig pushes on the mast foot will tend to make the board flip onto its side owing to the grip of the daggerboard. This is called "railing", and it is controlled by standing right out on the side of the board and carefully powering the rig. This technique is actually used by racers to enhance their speed upwind, as putting the board on edge makes it act like one long daggerboard.

Offwind, if the board is sailing at speed, the daggerboard must be fully retracted by kicking it up with your foot; if left down it will hydroplane and send you out of control.

Footstraps

Footstraps keep you connected to the board when bumping along over choppy water or waves at high speed. They allow you to exert maximum control over the board and at the same time to pull in on the rig. Long boards have double sets of footstraps; the front set are for sailing upwind, while the back set are for reaching — the windier it is, the more you move back to get as much of the board out of the water as possible.

Footstraps consist of a small loop of flexible material attached to the board at each end. They can cause injury if you fall with your feet still inside them, so you should always slide out of the straps as soon as you lose your balance.

Mast track

Most long boards are fitted with an adjustable sliding mast track, allowing you to adjust the position of the rig while sailing. You pull the rig right back to get the rig upright and as much of the board out of the water as possible when reaching at speed; you slide it forward when beating so that you can rake the rig back and sail in a more comfortable position.

Harness

The harness is without doubt the windsurfer's best friend. It allows you to hook in and hold onto a line on either side of the boom, taking the strain of hanging onto the rig with your whole body rather than just with your hands and arms. In stronger winds it extends your windsurfing time tenfold and more, and once the knack is learned it is easily mastered.

The traditional kind of harness is cut like a waist-coat, but most sailors now prefer lower waist or seat harnesses — the latter literally allows you to sit down while sailing.

Planing

The windsurfer's most rapid change in speed occurs when it stops sailing through the water like a yacht, and starts skimming *over* the water like a speedboat. This is called *planing* — with the right technique most boards will start planing in a Force 3, and really start to move fast in Force 4.

Planing calls for a different type of sailing. With the board skimming over the water you bank it like a ski to turn it, and forget steering with the rig; though to do this it has to be the right kind of design: narrow, with a low-volume tail. This technique is called "footsteering", allowing rapid changes in direction by putting weight on one side of the board or the other. It also leads to the *carve gybe* which is exclusively used to change tacks on short boards. Travelling fast, the sailor banks the board away from the wind, and continues to bank the board round onto its new course, flipping the rig and changing sides as he goes. This is a skilled manoeuvre which demands a lot of practice; the sailor aims to sail out of the gybe as fast as he sailed into it.

Footsteering is used to bank the board.

10
Wavesailing

No one has fully mastered windsurfing. There are always new tricks to learn and new techniques to master, and the weather has no time for fools.

Most advanced techniques involve short boards, and in particular sailing in waves. Wavesailing is based on surfing, which is how windsurfing was born. You sail out through the waves jumping as you go; ride back in with them; and perform "transitions" on the way.

Jumping

If a windsurfer hits a wave going fast it will take off into the air — it's just like a motor bike hitting a ramp. If it's going very fast and the ramp is long and steep it will also go very high, and jumps of up to 6 metres or more in the air can be performed by experts. While in the air there are many variations on the basic jump. The sailor can swing the board up over his head (this is called a "table top"), turn it round to the opposite direction in mid-air to perform an aerial gybe, or loop it end-over-end before landing safely.

Jumping off a wave face — great fun for the very experienced!

Obviously there is a certain degree of danger involved with the most extreme jumps. Falling on the board or rig, or having it fall onto you, can be painful, and in the biggest waves — such as those found at Hookipa on Maui — minor injuries and occasional fractures are not uncommon.

Riding

Riding in with a wave is a great sensation. The board travels incredibly fast, using the wind and the slope of the wave face to power it shorewards. At the best locations this technique is turned into a roller-coaster in which the sailor rides the full length of the wave, enjoying it all the way until it breaks in an explosion of foam.

Transitions

When the sailor gets to the bottom of the wave he will execute a "bottom turn" to sail back up it, travelling at very high speed. At the top of the wave he will "cut back" down the wave face, a rapid manoeuvre that redirects the board back onto the wave. In between he will be trying to avoid sailing through the breaking lip of the wave, and at the end of each ride will gybe on "the inside" to head back out through the waves, gybing on "the outside" when he's ready to ride back in with them again.

11

Windsurfing competition

Windsurfing competition takes place at local, national and international level, using a number of basic formats and events.

Course racing

Course racing is for long boards of around 3.70 m, carrying sails of up to 7.5 sq m. Typical examples of these boards are the Mistral Equipe, F2 World Cup Race, and Fanatic Cat. The competitors race around a course which includes beating, plenty of reaching, and plenty of gybes. In a local competition there is likely to be no minimum wind speed, but for official "Funboard" events the organisers demand a minimum wind speed of Force 4.

The Mistral '90 Equipe is ideal for course racing.

Slalom

Slalom is a high-speed competition for short boards in winds of Force 4 and above, usually run on a knock-out basis. At its simplest, eight boards race a few times around two buoys forming a figure-of-eight course.

They start — Le Mans style — on the beach, reach out, gybe, reach in, gybe again, and so on until the required number of laps are completed. The first four to finish go through to the next round.

The boards gybe round their mark in a slalom competition.

Wave performance

This is a knock-out short-board competition in which two sailors show off their wavesailing expertise, using every trick and manoeuvre they know in front of a panel of judges on the beach. After a set time the sailor with the best score wins and moves on to the next round.

Wave performance — one of the most exciting forms of competition

Speed

Speed events are held on 250- and 500-metre courses. Sailors enter the course singly with a flying start, and their recorded speeds are averages over the course. The prime requirements are very flat water and a lot of wind, and custom-made "speed needles" are used for this very specialised discipline. In 1990 the 500-metre world record was held by Frenchman Pascal Maka at 42.91 knots, making his board the fastest sailing craft ever!

1990 world speed champion Pascal Maka in action

Olympics

As from 1992, the windsurfing Olympics require Lechner Division 2 boards to be used. These have rounded hulls which are specially designed for sailing round an

Olympic Triangle, a course which places as much emphasis on beating and running as it does reaching, with no minimum wind speed. There are classes for both men and women.

One-designs

The best racing is often among "one-designs", where boards and rigs are exactly the same so that the sailor wins and not the equipment. The two leading classes are the Mistral One-Design and the Windsurfer Regatta based on Hoyle Schweitzer's original Windsurfer. As well as local events, there are national, European and world one-design championships.

Freestyle

Freestyle used to be a major part of all regattas, but has lost popularity in recent years. It's a solo long-board competition which is always good to watch, in which the sailor performs a number of tricks in a set time — pirouettes, duck tacks and gybes, riding "on the rail" (with the board flipped on its side), jumping through the boom, and many other variations. The performance is marked by a panel of judges.

World Tour

The Professional Boardsailors' Association organises windsurfing's most prestigious international series, comparable with similar events run for golf and tennis pros, though not with the same kind of prize money! Nevertheless, the top dozen or so sailors are extremely well paid by their sponsors to race on the World Tour, which has around 20 week-long events ranging round the world in locations as diverse as Japan, Hawaii, San Francisco, Aruba, Puerto Rico, France, Germany and Holland. Most of these events include the three official Funboard disciplines — course racing, slalom and wave performance. All of them have a minimum wind speed of Force 4.

World-class sailors are usually at their best in their early 20s. The top names to look out for at the time of writing are Bjørn Dunkerbeck, a naturalised Spaniard and twice World Champion; Robby Naish from Hawaii who was champion of champions for a decade until unseated by Dunkerbeck; Sweden's Anders Bringdal; France's Robert Teriitehau; Australia's Phil McGain; and a few others who will no doubt assert themselves in the years to come.

12
Top places

While windsurfers sail in almost every country, there are many places where conditions are anything but ideal — inconsistent wind, not enough waves, too cold a climate, etc. Britain suffers from inconsistency of wind and weather, but otherwise is well blessed with good wind-surfing conditions. However there are a small number of locations worldwide where conditions are excellent, and these are where the windsurfing migrants make for.

Hawaii

Without a doubt the mecca of windsurfing, Hawaii has the reputation, the top sailors, the wind, and a warm climate. Hawaii is composed of a chain of islands out in the Pacific far to the west of continental USA. The trade winds are consistently strong in summer and less consistent in winter, though as with all "windsurfing paradises" there are times when the wind switches off for days or even weeks on end. The main islands for wind-surfing are Oahu (the capital island) and Maui, which in recent years has succeeded Oahu in popularity. This is principally because Hookipa, the world's most famous wavesailing location, where huge waves break after travelling the breadth of the Pacific, is located on Maui.

The Canaries

The Canary Islands are sited in the Atlantic off the coast of North Africa. For Europeans they offer cheap holidays, winter sun, and good windsurfing conditions. In the winter the wind is variable but can be excellent; in the summer the trade winds are boosted by the thermal effect of the sun and warm land, and good windsurfing weather is usually the order of the day. Most windsurfing is done on Lanzarote and on the relatively unpopulated Fuerteventura, which also boasts some very good wavesailing. There are also popular spots on Gran Canaria (at Bahia Feliz), and on Tenerife (at El Medano).

Making a deep-water start in tropical waters

Western Australia

No round-up of the world's best windsurfing spots would be complete without a mention of Western Australia, which offers conditions as good as Hawaii's but without the crowds. The best known places include Geraldton, Lancelin and Margaret River, all within striking distance of WA's main city of Perth. The Australian summer (Europe's winter) has the best wind and weather.

Other places

In the western Mediterranean, on the southern tip of Spain, Tarifa boasts very strong summer winds funnelled through the Straits of Gibraltar and is a favourite with short-board sailors. Further east the north of Sardinia has good summer winds, while at the other end of the Mediterranean the Greek islands and some of the Turkish mainland offer a variety of specialist windsurfing holiday centres, generally getting windier the further east you go.

In the Atlantic south of the Canaries, the Cape Verde islands are a recently discovered windsurfing hotspot offering wind, big waves and sun in unspoiled surroundings. There is not much of a tourist industry, which some would consider a blessing, but the islands are expensive to get to.

On the other side of the Atlantic much of the Caribbean has good trade-wind conditions, sometimes with waves to match. Favourite locations include Barbados, Puerto Rico, Aruba and Belize.

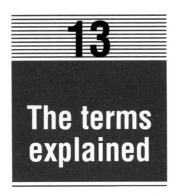

13

The terms explained

Windsurfing has a language of its own which at first may seem complex and difficult to understand. The glossary which follows is by no means complete, but it should set you up with most of the common and not-so-common terms that you're likely to come up against.

All-round Used to describe a board or sail that is suitable for all-round use — meaning both light and strong winds, or different sea conditions.

Apparent wind The apparent wind is the wind as you feel it while sailing. Its speed is a combination of that of the *true wind* plus (sailing upwind) or minus (sailing downwind) the speed of your board.

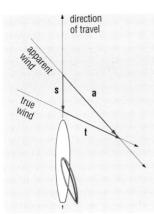

Figure 14 The apparent wind **a** is a combination of the true wind **t** and the "wind of the board's own speed" **s**. If you know the actual speeds and directions of **s** and **t**, you can work out the apparent wind by drawing a triangle as shown here, where the sides of the triangle are proportional to the speeds.

Battens Lengths of flexible glassfibre that support the shape in the sail. Battens are either full length or short.

Bearing away Altering course away from the direction the wind is blowing from.

Beating Sailing as close as possible to the direction the wind is blowing from, by tacking in a zigzag course.

Boardsailing Another name for windsurfing, as is *sailboarding*.

Boom Metal tubing covered in a soft grip, usually connected to the mast by a clamp, and featuring an arrangement of pulleys and clamps at the rear (clew) end to attach it to the sail.

Bow see *nose*.

Buoyancy aid A flotation waistcoat that will keep you afloat in the water. You should use a buoyancy aid while learning.

Camber The amount of depth or "belly" in a sail.

Carve Carving a turn or carving a gybe is altering course at high speed by banking the board like a ski.

Centre of Effort (CE) The balance point in the sail where the wind's power acts as though it is concentrated.

Centre of Lateral Resistance (CLR) The balance point of a board about which it turns — on a long board the CLR is around the daggerboard.

Chop Small wind-blown waves.

Cleat A small fitting used to secure a line. Windsurfers use a self-jamming cleat to secure the outhaul or downhaul.

Clew The outer or back corner of the sail which is attached to the far end of the boom.

Clew-first Sailing along with the sail reversed and the clew pointing into the wind.

Close-hauled Sailing as close to the wind as possible.

Concaves Boards have all kinds of bottom shapes, and many incorporate single, double, triple or more concaves designed to promote speed.

Cross-shore or **sideshore** A wind blowing across your launch point; this is best for windsurfing, giving you the possibility of a beam reach out and a beam reach back.

Daggerboard The big removable fin in the middle of the board which stops it going sideways when you are sailing upwind. Offwind when sailing at speed you retract the daggerboard, as otherwise it can make the board difficult to control. See chapter 9.

Downhaul Modern sails are usually tuned by downhaul tension — that is, pulling on the bottom of the sail.

Dumper A wave that breaks fiercely on a steeply shelving shoreline, often with a dangerous undertow.

Fin The fin or skeg allows the tail to grip the water and keep the board travelling straight.

Foot The bottom of the sail. The *mastfoot* is the fitting that connects the rig to the board.

Footsteering When the board is planing, you put weight on the side furthest away from you (leeward rail) or the side nearest you (windward rail) to make the board bear off or head up to the wind. See chapter 9.

Footstraps Straps to put your feet into so that you stay connected to the board. They are only necessary in stronger winds. See chapter 9.

Freestyle This involves performing fancy tricks and manoeuvres on a board; see chapter 11.

Funboard A generic term for a board that's at its best in stronger winds. See chapter 2.

Gybing Altering course through 180 degrees so that the tail of the board passes through the eye of the wind.

Harness The windsurfer's best friend! It's used to hook into a harness line fixed to create a loop on either side of the boom, taking the strain off your arms. There are three basic styles: seat, waist and chest harnesses.

Head The top of the sail.

Head up Alter course towards the wind, achieved in lighter winds by inclining the rig over the tail, and in stronger winds by footsteering.

Heel When a board or rig leans over, it is said to *heel*.

High aspect ratio A term borrowed from aerodynamics. A sail or fin of high aspect ratio is tall and narrow, whereas a low aspect one is short and squat.

Hull The basic board, excluding the rig.

The final stages in manufacturing a low-cost hull of the polythene-skin type

Inhaul The inhaul line attaches the boom to the mast; in most cases it is now superseded by a clamp system.

IYRU The International Yacht Racing Union is responsible for the Olympic Class and International Flatboard Class.

Knots Nautical miles per hour. A nautical mile is 2,025 yards (1.85 km) rather than the more familiar 1,760 yards (1.61 km).

Leash A line connecting the rig to the board in case the mastfoot comes adrift is a wise precaution.

Lee A lee shore has an onshore wind, so the shore is on the leeward of your board.

Leeward The side the wind is blowing away from; the sheltered side.

Leeway The amount a board slips sideways.

Leech The edge of the sail between the head and the clew.

Luff The "front" edge of the sail from the head to the tack. The luff tube connects the sail to the mast. *Luffing* is sailing up towards the wind.

Mast Most masts are made of glassfibre, though those for racing are more often made of aluminium which is lighter and stiffer. Standard-length masts are either 465 cm or 485 cm, and can be extended for use with larger sails by the addition of an adjustable mast extension. See chapter 3.

Mastfoot or **mast base** This connects the rig to the board via a universal joint which allows 360-degree rotation of the rig. See chapter 3.

Mast track A sliding track mounted in the board, operated by a pedal, and allowing the rig to be moved backwards and forwards for different wind conditions. See chapter 7.

Monofilm A see-through sailcloth which has become popular in recent years.

Nose or **bow** The front of the board.

Olympic Triangle The traditional IYRU race course for yachts and dinghies, which is also used in some windsurfing events. The course has three legs with corners forming an equilateral triangle. For most windsurfing the more modern "M"-shaped course is preferred.

One-design A few boards are raced as identical "one-designs" — the Windsurfer Regatta, the Mistral One-Design, and on occasions the Bic Bamba. See chapter 11.

Outhaul Line to pull the clew of the sail out to the end of the boom.

Planing Skimming across the top of the water, rather than sailing through it as a ship or yacht does.

Port The left side (looking forward), indicated in nautical circles by the colour red.

Pumping Pumping the rig back and forth creates wind in the sail and gets a board going faster in lighter airs. It is a technique used in racing, but banned in many regattas.

Rail The sides of the board — just think of riding on rails. Rail shape and design is an important factor in how a board performs. Rails are sometimes described as "hard" (flat with sharp edges), or "soft" (round).

Railing Sailing fast with the daggerboard down, a board will tend to heel over and ride up on its edge. This technique can be used to sail much faster upwind.

Reaching Sailing with the wind blowing onto the side of the board. If you're sailing perpendicular to the wind it's a beam reach; with the wind coming slightly from in front of you it's a close reach; with the wind coming from slightly behind it's a broad reach. Broad reaching is the fastest course of all. See chapter 8.

Rig The mast, sail, boom and mastfoot combined.

Roach The area of the sail which is supported by battens outside a straight line running from head to clew.

Rocker The curve in the nose and tail of a board, when viewed from the side. Rocker is necessary to lift the board up and over the chop; a flat board with no rocker would submarine into every tiny wave. Too much rocker, however, makes a board slow and difficult to get going.

Rotational A popular sail design in which full-length tapered battens are used to push the sail round to the leeward side of the board on each tack to promote smooth airflow.

Running Running downwind is sailing with the wind behind you, a course least used by windsurfers, as it is both slow and wobbly.

Sailboarding Another name for windsurfing, as is *boardsailing*.

Scoop Another name for nose *rocker.*

Sinker A low-volume short board without enough buoyancy to float while carrying a sailor. The lift from the wind in the sail stops them from actually sinking while sailing at speed.

Skeg Another word for the tail *fin.*

Slot The slot is the gap between the foot of the sail and the deck. Closing the slot makes a windsurfer go faster.

Slot flusher or **gasket** Two strips of plastic which keep the water out of the daggerboard case.

Spin-out Travelling very fast on a reach puts a lot of pressure on the fin. It may suddenly lose its grip, causing the tail to slide away, which is called spin-out.

Spreader bar An aluminium bar which spreads the load taken by the harness.

Starboard The right side (looking forward), indicated by the colour green in nautical circles.

Tack The corner of the sail.

Tacking Altering course so that the nose of the board passes through the eye of the wind. See also *beating*.

Tail or **stern** The back of the board.

True wind The wind as experienced by a stationary observer. See also *apparent wind*.

Universal joint The UJ or "powerjoint" is a rubber or mechanical coupling between the bottom of the mast and the mastfoot, which allows a windsurfer rig to be swung in any direction.

Uphaul A thick rope used to pull up or uphaul the rig.

Volume The volume of a board determines its buoyancy, its weight-carrying ability, and to some extent its speed.

Waterstart Allowing the wind in the sail to lift you out of the water — the only way to start a *sinker*. It's not as easy as it might look.

Wave board A specialist short board used for wavesailing (see chapter 10). Waveboards are generally very short (less than 270 cm), and well rockered to turn easily and prevent nosediving.

Windsurfer Strictly speaking, a Windsurfer with a capital W was the original Windsurfer conceived and produced by Hoyle Schweitzer. All the rest are windsurfers, and we all go windsurfing. The sailor on the board is also sometimes called a windsurfer.

Windward The side (of the board) the wind is blowing onto.

Wishbone Old-fashioned name for the *boom*.

World Tour The international funboard regatta circuit run by the PBA (Professional Boardsailors' Association), sometimes called the World Cup. See chapter 11.

Useful addresses

Great Britain

RYA Windsurfing
Royal Yachting Association
RYA House
Romsey Road
Eastleigh
Hampshire
SO5 4YA

RYA Windsurfing runs Britain's National Windsurfing Scheme which offers five levels of tuition for adults and a special scheme for children (see chapter 5). It provides free windsurfing information; is responsible for training potential Olympic windsurfers; and guards the right of windsurfers to free water access.

UK Boardsailing Association (UKBSA)
Masons Road
Stratford-upon-Avon
Warwickshire
CV37 9NZ

The UK Boardsailing Association runs a popular series of national and local regattas. Help and advice can be given to anyone interested in taking up racing.

British Windsurfing Association (BWA)
163 West Lane
Hayling Island
Hampshire
PO11 0JW

The British Windsurfing Association runs the British Funboard Cup national series of Force 4+ course racing and slalom events. It also administers British Speed Association events, held on 250-metre courses at half a dozen UK locations.

Overseas

In general, the same bodies administer windsurfing as sailing.

Australian Yachting Federation
33 Peel Street
Milson's Point
NSW 2061
Australia

Canadian Yachting Association
1600 James Naismith Drive
Gloucester
Ontario
K1B 5N4
Canada

New Zealand Yachting Federation
PO Box 4173
Auckland 1
New Zealand

United States Yacht Racing Union
PO Box 209
Newport
RI 02840
USA

International

Professional Boardsailors' Association (PBA)
1 Barn Cottages
Albany Park
Colnbrook
Slough
SL3 0HS

The Professional Boardsailors' Association administers the PBA series of international funboard events around the world.

International Yacht Racing Union (IYRU)
60 Knightsbridge
London
SW1 7JX

The International Yacht Racing Union administers all Olympic windsurfing competition, as well as Funboard and Production Class racing.